Ways We Go

We Go on an Airplane

by Joanne Mattern

LOOK! BOOKS™

Red Chair Press Egremont, Massachusetts

Look! Books are produced and published by Red Chair Press:
Red Chair Press LLC PO Box 333 South Egremont, MA 01258-0333
www.redchairpress.com

FREE Educator Guides at www.redchairpress.com/free-resources

Publisher's Cataloging-in-Publication Data
Names: Mattern, Joanne, 1963–
Title: We go on an airplane / by Joanne Mattern.
Other Titles: Airplane

Description: Egremont, Massachusetts : Red Chair Press, [2019] | Series: Look! books. Ways we go | Includes glossary and "Good to Know" fact boxes. | Interest age level: 004-007. | Includes bibliographical references and index. | Summary: "What to expect from a trip on an airplane."--Provided by publisher.

Identifiers: ISBN 9781634406321 (library hardcover) | ISBN 9781634406444 (paperback) | ISBN 9781634406383 (ebook) | LCCN 2018955665

Subjects: LCSH: Transportation--Juvenile literature. | Airplanes--Juvenile literature. | CYAC: Transportation. | Airplanes.

Classification: LCC HE152 .M381 2019 (print) | LCC HE152 (ebook) | DDC 388 [E]--dc23

Photo credits: All iStock except for the following: pp. 1, 3, 9, 11, 19 Shutterstock; pp. 16–17 Alamy.

Printed in United States of America

0519 1P CGF19

Table of Contents

A First Airplane Trip

Many people fly on airplanes. There is a lot to do to get ready to fly. Let's take off and see what it is like to go on an airplane!

Good to Know

The first building you will go to is called a terminal.

Flying Suitcases

It is good to get to the airport early. First you will give your suitcases to a worker at the airport. Big suitcases fly in the **cargo hold** of the plane. You can carry small cases on board.

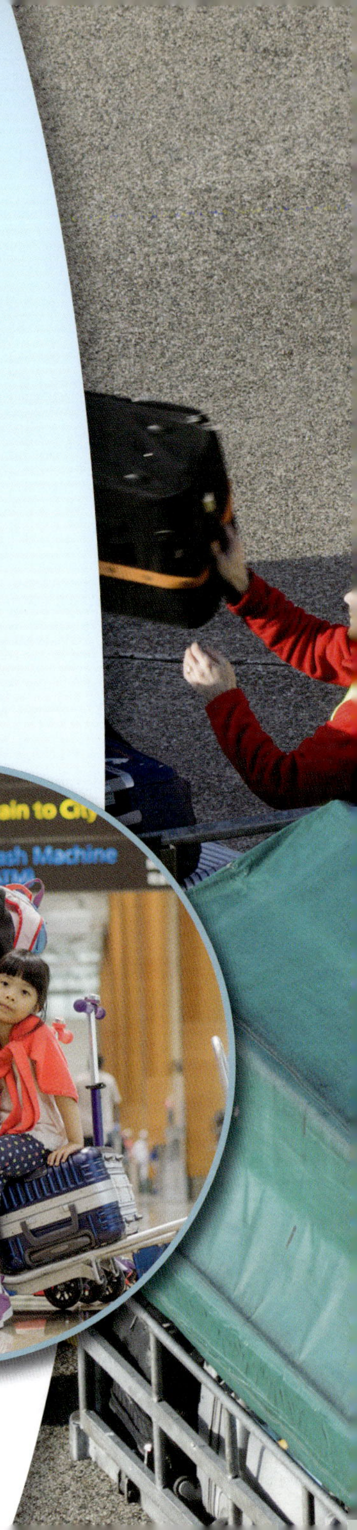

The people who take cases on and off the plane are specially trained to handle the baggage.

Staying Safe

Next people go through **security**. A worker will look through your bags. **Passengers** have to walk through a **metal detector**. Sometimes you have to take off your shoes.

That's funny!

Waiting to Fly

Next you have to find your **gate**. People wait there until their flight is ready. You might see your plane waiting outside.

Planes are cleaned and bags are loaded while you wait at the gate.

It's time to go! Passengers show their **boarding passes** to a worker at the gate. Then you walk down a long **jetway** to get on the plane.

Take Off!

When you get on the airplane, you must fasten your seat belt. Then it is time to take off. The plane drives down the **runway** very fast. Then—zoom! You are in the air!

Good to Know

Two people drive the plane, a pilot and co-pilot.

In the Air

The flight might be short or long. On long flights, you might watch a movie or sleep. You can eat snacks too.

Good to Know

The people who work in a plane are there to help you.

On the Ground

The **pilot** will say when it is time to land. Click! We made sure our seat belts were on. The plane flies down, down, down. Then there is a big bump. The plane is on the ground!

Everyone lines up to get off the plane. Most passengers go to a special room to get their suitcases. Then it is time to meet family or get a ride to a hotel. Your first plane ride is over!

Words to Know

boarding passes: papers that let people go on an airplane

cargo hold: part of an airplane that holds suitcases and other large objects

gate: the door that leads from the airport to the airplane

jetway: a bridge that connects the airport gate to the door of the airplane

metal detector: a machine that senses if a person is carrying metal objects

passengers: people who travel in a vehicle

pilot: person who controls a plane

runway: a long flat area where airplanes take off and land

security: people who check to make sure everything is safe

Learn More at the Library

Books (Check out these books to learn more.)

Adamson, Thomas K. *Airplanes.* Bellwether Media, 2017.

Brown, Carron. *On the Plane.* Kane Miller, 2016.

Brown, Jordan. *How Airplanes Get From Here...to There.* Simon Spotlight, 2016.

Manushkin, Fran. *Fly High, Katie.* Picture Window Books, 2014.

Index

About the Author

Joanne Mattern has written hundreds of nonfiction books for children. She likes writing about different people and places. Joanne lives in New York State with her family.